Summer Bulbs

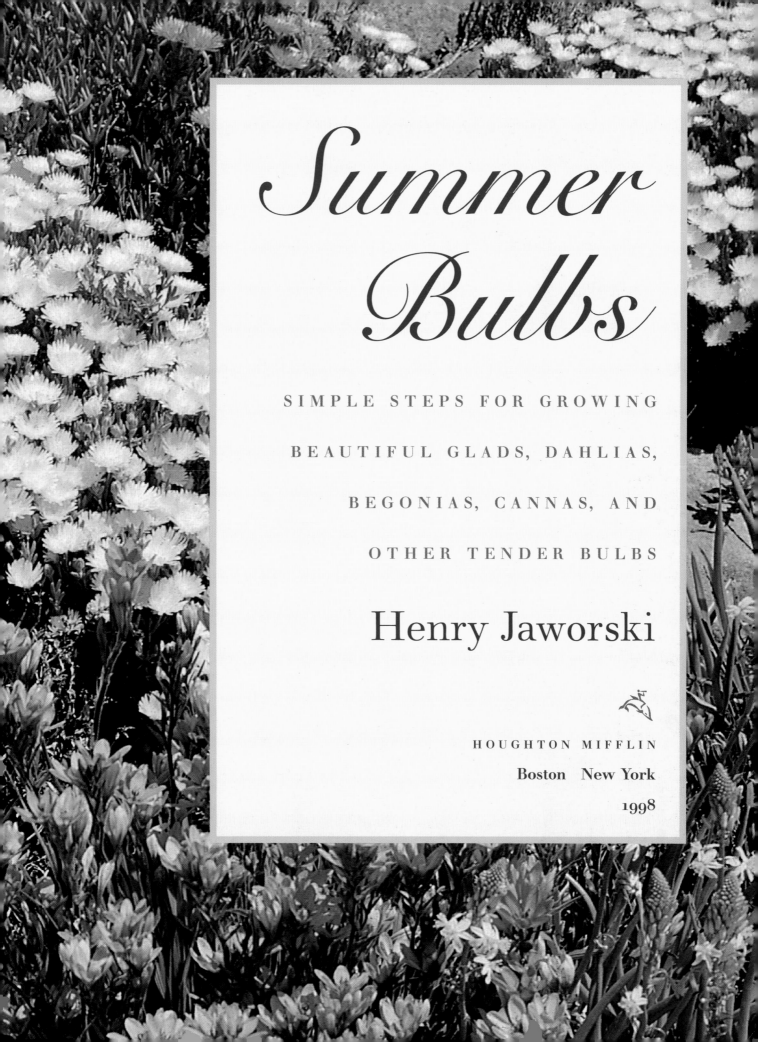

Summer Bulbs

SIMPLE STEPS FOR GROWING BEAUTIFUL GLADS, DAHLIAS, BEGONIAS, CANNAS, AND OTHER TENDER BULBS

Henry Jaworski

HOUGHTON MIFFLIN

Boston   New York

1998

(On title page): Babiana stricta and Lampranthus

(Right): Begonia × tuberhybrida

For information about permissions to
reproduce selections from this book, write to Permissions,
215 Park Avenue South, New York, NY 10003.

Library of Congress Cataloging-in-Publication Data
Jaworksi, Henry, date.
Summer bulbs : simple steps for growing beautiful glads,
dahlias, begonias, cannas, and other tender
bulbs / Henry Jaworski.
p. cm.
Includes bibliographical references (p.   ) and index.
ISBN 0-395-89261-9
1. Bulbs. I. Title.
SB425.J37 1998
635.9 4—dc21   98-11775   CIP

Printed in the United States of America

10 9 8 7 6 5 4 3 2 1

Cover photo by Alain Masson
Book design and composition by Anne Chalmers